OUR EARTH

Written and illustrated by

ANNE ROCKWELL

CLARION BOOKS
An Imprint OF HarperCollins*Publishers*
Boston New York

Our earth is where I live.

It is a big, round globe.

It has a frozen North Pole at the top
and an icy cold South Pole at the bottom.

Our earth was shaped by water, fire, ice,
and living things. It is always changing—
much too slowly for us to see.

Once our earth was covered with warm water.
Some dinosaurs lived in its warm and ferny swamps.
Then our earth turned cold.

Huge sheets of slowly moving ice called glaciers crept across the earth and wore rocks smooth. Glaciers are still moving in places on our earth.

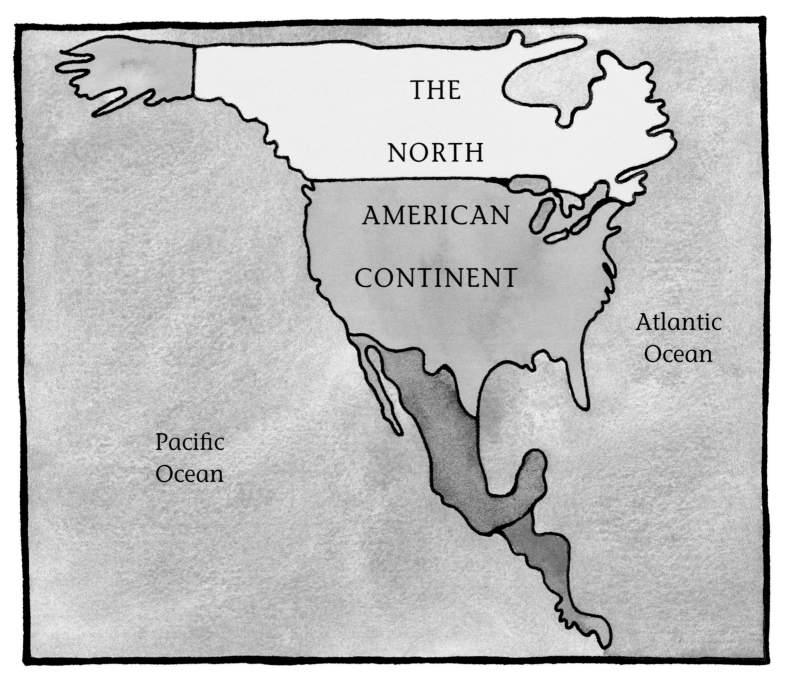

The biggest pieces of land on earth are continents.
Their shorelines meet the sea.

Islands are smaller pieces of land
that rise up out of the sea.

Some islands are born when volcanoes erupt
below the sea. Hot lava cools, and over time
it turns to soil where green things can grow.

Some islands are coral reefs that grow and grow
until they poke above the water,
and birds bring seeds to them.

Water gushing up from the ground, and rain,
and melted snow, fills streams, ponds, and lakes.

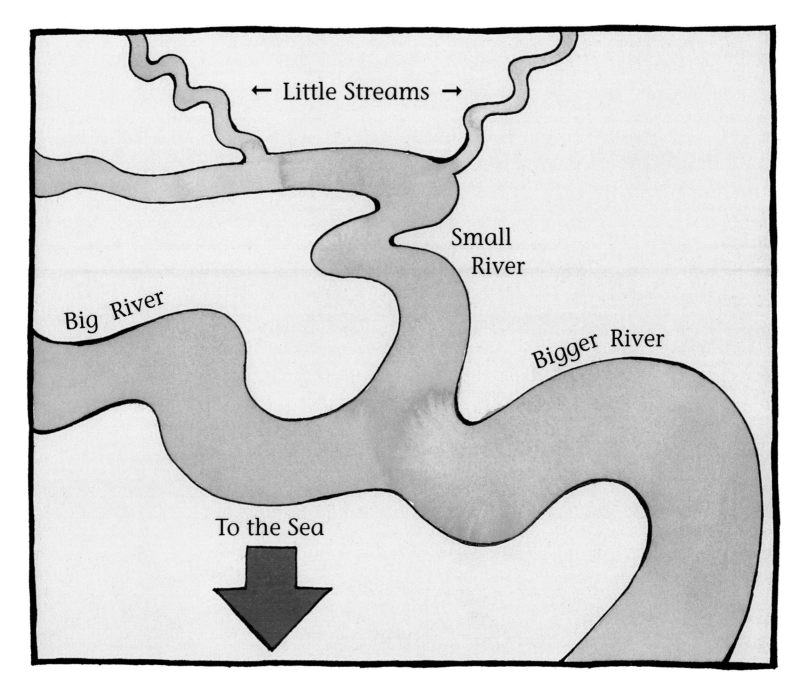

Streams flow into small rivers,
which flow into bigger ones.

Nothing can stop water from finding its way.

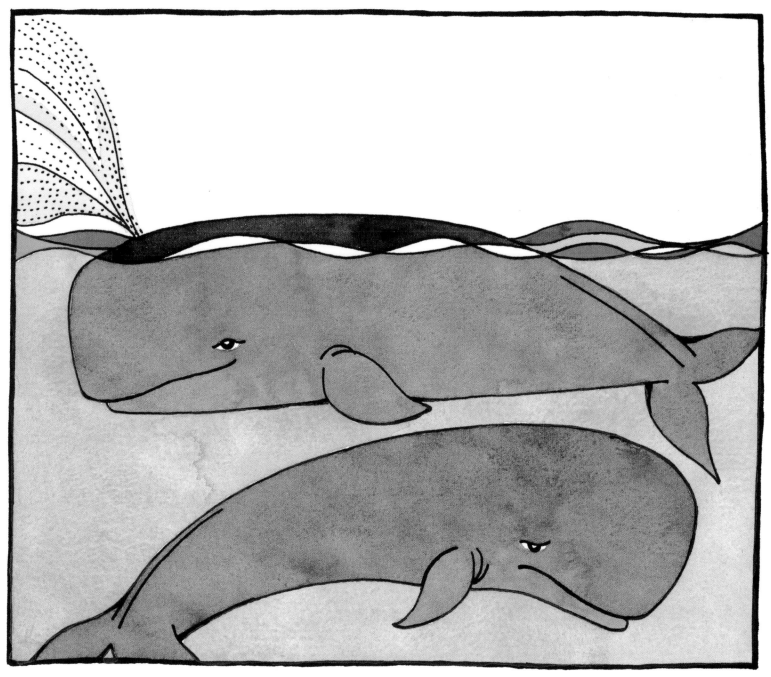

Some rivers dry up and stop flowing.
But some empty into the salty sea.

The land on our earth has rounded hills
that enclose green valleys.

There are many forests on our earth.
Rain forests are full of flowers, and birds,
and monkeys jumping through green-leafed trees.

There are hot, sandy deserts
where lizards live and prickly cacti grow.

There are dark, damp caves
that go far down into the earth.

There are tall canyons carved by years
and years of rushing water.

There are high, snowcapped mountains
reaching up to the clouds in the sky.

Our big, round earth is very beautiful.

It is my home and yours.

For
Christian Rockwell Brion

www.harpercollinschildrens.com

Library of Congress Cataloging-in-Publication Data
Rockwell, Anne F.
Our earth/Anne Rockwell.
p. cm.
Summary: A simple introduction to geography which explains such things as how the earth
was shaped, how islands are born from volcanoes, and how gushing springs affect rivers.
1. Geography—Juvenile literature.   [1. Geography.]   I. Title.
G133.R63   1998
910—dc21   97-1247
ISBN 978-0-15-201679-1
ISBN 978-0-15-202383-6 pb

23 RRDA 35 34 33 32 31 30
Printed in Malaysia

The illustrations in this book were done in watercolor and gouache on paper.
The display type was set in Schwere.
The text type was set in Stone Informal.
Color separations by Tien Wah Press, Singapore
Production supervision by Stanley Redfern and Pascha Gerlinger
Designed by Linda Lockowitz